A Color Rose!

A COLOR ROSE!

Cheronne Romy Roberts

RESOURCE *Publications* • Eugene, Oregon

A COLOR ROSE!

Copyright © 2024 Cheronne Romy Roberts. All rights reserved. Except for brief quotations in critical publications or reviews, no part of this book may be reproduced in any manner without prior written permission from the publisher. Write: Permissions, Wipf and Stock Publishers, 199 W. 8th Ave., Suite 3, Eugene, OR 97401.

Resource Publications
An Imprint of Wipf and Stock Publishers
199 W. 8th Ave., Suite 3
Eugene, OR 97401

www.wipfandstock.com

PAPERBACK ISBN: 979-8-3852-0863-0
HARDCOVER ISBN: 979-8-3852-0864-7
EBOOK ISBN: 979-8-3852-0865-4

VERSION NUMBER 03/27/24

Contents

Winter

A Color Rose | 3
The Way Home | 4
Usual Stranger | 5
Renounce | 6
Decompose | 7
Cancer | 8
Jane Doe | 9
The City of Souls | 11
Freedom of Speech | 12

Autumn Fall

A Beggar | 17
War | 19
Armageddon | 21
The Black Bird Crow | 22
Forever Like Gold | 23
Life | 25
The Black Horseman | 26
Destiny | 27
The Black Butterfly | 28
Asphyxia | 29
Uncharted River | 30
Confessions | 31

Save Me from Myself | 33
Goodbye | 35
Heaven | 36
Unbroken | 37
Saving Grace | 38
Deaf Praying | 40

Spring

Valentine | 43
Cardiac Arrest | 44
Beautiful Sin | 45
Envious | 47
Love Letter in A Glass | 48
Insomnia | 49
Bullet | 50
Suicide | 52
Pseudonym | 53
Cold Case | 54
Dissect | 55
The Dead | 56
The Graveyard | 57
No Sympathy | 58
Crying Wolf | 60
Mr.Narcissist | 61

Summer

The Cape Troupes | 65
Set Me Free | 67
Silence | 68
Victory | 69
Champion | 70
Powerful | 71
Alive! | 72

Bibliography | 73

Winter

A Color Rose

In the midst of a cold winter in 1953
Living in the segregation of color and poverty
A town called the city by the sea
The Cape, District 6, is a colorful community.

Classified as non-white, either black, or merely two syllables in-between
In social housing, there is a girl named Rose, aged only thirteen.
Reminded of her class every day with the apartheid regime
To feel free and human was her true, unspoken dream.

Down on the shoreline, designated for the underprivileged family
She collects marine debris and seashells for art and history.
Overshadowed by the rocks and among the ocean breeze
She found solace in being alone and felt an inner peace.

Confronted by a blue uniform and gold badge worn by three
Demanded by their guns to get on her knees
Raped and silenced, then bruised for her pleas
Finding the humor in her agony as she bleeds

After impregnating her with a racist seed,
The white policemen then threw her into the dirty streets.
With no laws enforcing justice for such evil deeds
Since violating only white women was punishable as a sin,
It was not deemed a crime to rape women with a different color of skin!

The Way Home

The cheap smell of a brandy bought from the south
Is now drenched in gray on the beard of his mouth.
As he waits for his stepdaughter in an empty house
The creak of the backdoor breaks the silence aloud.

As she attempts to elude the sky in the dark as a cloud
She hides in her closet and prays that she is never found.
With every stride of echoed footsteps on the ground
She was closer to hell as the devil hunted her down.

In a shattered innocence forever to be bound
She pauses the world and mutes all of its sound.
She will never scream, and she will never shout.
No, she is not brave, and she is not proud.
For she knows the monster feeds on
All of her fears and all of her doubts.

She stares out her window until the daylight is gone.
And when the cold mist of the night finds her alone,
She runs, stumbling to the river like a sorrowful song.
As autumn would fall and the winters would drown

She lays afloat on the crest like pearls from a crown.
White as an angel on a bed of beautiful stones
With a note that reads in a writing of her own
"Always follow the stream to find your way home!"

Usual Stranger

The gush of the wind embraces
Every staggering step she takes
While she recognizes an old stranger's face
As he often reads the newspaper on Mondays,

Among all the colors, she seemed to be the only gray.
As she stood frozen in the middle of the busy subway
She franticly walked up to a priest and asked him to pray.
Then he anxiously washed his hands as she walked away.
As she ran down to hell, stumbling onto the railway

She sat facing north on the coal seams.
As she hears the rattling steel and the train steam
With a ghostly stare, while still searching for her dreams.
She greeted her death with such horrific screams.

A silence fell upon her as she no longer breathed.
Muting the noisy train station and one million feet
Then guilt engulfed the crowd like a fire of regret.
For recognizing the usual stranger now only in her death
Tormented by this truth, which will always reflect
Ironically, now her face they will never forget.

Renounce

The scent of a fresh casserole still lingers in the air.
While family portraits are scattered everywhere,
As her daughters wipe the blood from her hair,
Gun to his own temple, he has more bullets than tears.

Then the sound of a distressed flare.
Left a shuddering echo in their ears.
With a thud, their father fell from the kitchen chair.
They failed to recognize their mother, no matter how they stared.
Beaten to her death, they wondered if she was scared.

Her eyes swollen blue as her body lay bare.
New and old wounds tell the tales of her warfare.
If only she knew, she was stronger than all of her fears.
She would still be alive, sharpening all of her spears.

If she knew her worth was deeper than her scars,
She could have saved herself from her broken heart.
As she evolves into dust in the sky, like a falling star,
The tragedy left her daughters in a world so dark.
Now they will surely renounce love, and they will surely renounce God!

Decompose

Hidden behind her smile is a broken soul.
It was so damaged that it could not be sold.
Her heart has been flat-lined for so long that it has been cold.
Killed by the silence of the stories she never told,

In a world where sin is bartered for diamonds and gold,
She prays to rather walk on water than on coals.
She keeps fighting to see heaven, for she knows
When the darkness falls upon her, hell becomes too close.

In a thorned garden, she is like a winter rose.
She would always attempt to harvest her field, although it froze.
If you find her heart, this is a love she will always hold.
Though her love is a weakness that she could never show,

In life, we become overshadowed by demons that we never chose.
Like the beautiful violins of death that she was born to compose
Now her truth is like her spirit hidden behind her bones.
Her buried tragedies she would rather die than expose

Thus, she snorts her depression, then dies from the overdose.
For her anticipated suicide, no suspicion arose.
Since it was evident long before her death, she had begun
to decompose.

Cancer

Stalking her like a shadow in her life
Haunting her in the middle of the night
Like a cannibal consuming her from inside.
Overpowering her like the strongest tide

Amidst this impending death, she can no longer be blind.
Appearing as the living dead to everyone who has sight.
Within her own skin, she can no longer hide.
As she realizes she is losing this fight,

Since it is too late for any doctor or knife,
Now she mourns as a daughter, mother, and wife.
As there is no price that could ever buy time,
She accepts that she is already waiting in line.

Soon, the angels will call her to the light.
Now all she can do is prepare for the flight.
As she tends to her wings stroking the hide
She realizes that as long as she is breathing, her cancer is alive.
And the only way to defeat this disease is to die!

Jane Doe

In the midst of winter, at 12 in the dark
He flashes his lights and waits in his car.
On the street corner in front of the bar
She waits for a client to charge.

Trafficked away from home now so far
Smoking the city up like a cigar
He calls her over to his jaguar.
She climbs in and suggests a park.

On the back seat, it all happened too fast.
Victim to rape with a sentence to death as the cost.
She begged for heroin and money from her boss.
Now homeless on the street, pregnant, and lost

Addicted to ice, snow, and the frost
With every high, she tried to forget her past.
Overdosing on the pavement underneath the stars
She counted how long the contractions would last.

She found an alley west of four blocks.
Then she gave birth in the dumpster at 2 o'clock.
She cut the cord and left her baby with kisses so soft.
Then she abandoned him to die in an old rag and dirty cloth.

Back to the streets to put food in her mouth
As she infects the city from north to south.
She tries to escape, but her fate is bound.
She kneels at the gravesite where her son was found.

Desperately tightens the noose from a rope and slips it around.
As she vacantly emptied her eyes, she made not one sound.
She prays to God and promises herself to never look down.
Then she ran into the darkness, embracing all of her fears
with her feet off the ground!

The City of Souls

Greeted by the hands of murder
Out on the corner
Where nobody can win
Sons killing mothers
Then injecting the sin
Daughters take pride in selling their skin.
Abandoning her baby to decay inside a bin.
We are all on death row, awaiting the end.
When each sunrise brings poverty again,
Snorted until blurred and minds are bent
Then rob the next to pay for your rent.
Our freedom is paid for at such a great cost.
In a city where all our souls are lost.

Freedom of Speech

In a land where extortion leaves a nation destitute,
We have the voting power to elect who constitutes
If only, through our ignorance, we understood
One voice, if united, is louder and more powerful.
Than the corrupt hands of politicians hired to rule.

Imprisoned by poverty and too oblivious to the truth
We pay for our civil rights to be abused.
States gain riches by pickpocketing the impoverished for jewels.
We are compliant with being robbed if we never dispute.

Immune to crime, even the white collars are rotting at the root.
Forced to live with murderers in gang-infested neighborhoods
While the father who raped then killed his own daughter at age two
Will be released on bail and back at home in time for her funeral.

With the death penalty abolished and long overdue
We are starved for real justice, and it will always allude
If the system still protects the rights of a criminal,
Treating the life of a victim as an expired warranty and unvaluable.

We are stripped of our dignity until we are completely nude.
If being deprived of one human right classifies us as animals,
Yet to acknowledge that we have long been subdued.
As unenlightened as a power outage with no coal or crude

In a society where it seems like a more serious crime to loot,
We are left discouraged from painting the town blue.
Unable to eliminate human trafficking, then failing to prosecute
Now children are killed and kidnapped for their organs at school.
Women are abducted, turned into sex slaves, and forced to prostitute.

Now we live contently silenced by these institutes.
We tolerate these violations, and we misconstrue.
We were never really free if we accepted this as true.
With our future dead and now killing the dreams of our youth,
While being more concerned with the laces of a tourist shoe
Ignorant to the many thorns in the heel of a citizen's foot!

Autumn Fall

A Beggar

There, in the midst of death and fate
In a line where the third class awaits
Where every beggar clings to the pearly gates
And all the homeless still have an empty plate.

Once there, the old man said,
"Have mercy on me, for God's sake!
For we are the fallen, we are the disgraced,
I have traveled so far just to see God's face.

To lay my head down, is there some place?
We have only been living to be passing days.
For neither water nor food have I remembered the taste.
For my son, he needs your favor, and he needs your grace."

There stood an angel with a papyrus page.
Where his name was once inscribed and is now erased.
With a sorrowful heart, the old man walked away.
He then paused as he heard his son say
"Oh, father, please do not cry.
For my sins were carried with pride,
And all of my demons I kept alive.
Feeding off of my soul all of this time
Will now be the cost of my eternal life.

I pray you soon to find
A peace within God as we say goodbye
Now gently wipe your beautiful eyes.
I ask the angels only to light up the sky.
As we stand lost now by side
It seems so sudden to realize
I am merely a beggar standing outside.
The gates of heaven tonight!"

War

A Victorian English rose sits under the oak tree.
With a letter stained with Virginian tea
Sealing the burned envelope with a photograph in-between
Gazing out at the sunset far beyond the horizon at sea

She reminisces about the last time her soldier was seen
Down in the chapel, at only sixteen
He is now 32 and still at war with foreign marines.
She stares down at her beautiful vintage wedding ring.

Of age and too eager for his war story to begin.
Her son vows to find where his father has been.
With her letter in hand and a camo uniform of olive green
He flies over the Atlantic with iron fighter wings.

In the midst of the nuclear smoke, like a desolate dream
He walks into the baron field, where the dead now sing.
The soldiers alive hear only hellish screams.
Too young to inhale rotten flesh like a sunflower in spring

He kneels down in agony and prays to his king.
He hears the distinct sound of a landmine pin.
A soldier nearby rushes to the grisly scene.
The boy dies in his arms while staring up to heaven.

The soldier closes his eyes and gently lays him down to sleep.
Anticipatingly tugging off the young boy's tags to identify who he is,
In a loud silence, the inherited name dawned upon him.
Resonating in the wake of this tragic truth, he soon realizes
He is a father to a son he never recognized, and a stranger to
his own kin!

Armageddon

Fallen stars from the sky
Down onto burning flames
All the mountains are covered with tides.
Bringing an end to all the days

Hell explodes as the devil's lava rises.
Flooding the earth like canvas paint
Now the loud and chaotic prayers and cries
Are unheard by every angel and every saint.

The dead are now resurrected and alive.
With the cost of sin soon to be weighed,
Every soul has a tagged price.
For immortality to be paid.

Hunted by a dragon with seven eyes
Will he remember my name?
As the wicked and evil are all set alight,
On this judgment day,

In the darkness of the night
There is just an empty stage.
For he who holds the keys to death and life,
Will I recognize his face?

The Black Bird Crow

Lost in a world where the dead have no souls
Seen burning angels with no halo's
I have been drowning in a room with no windows.
Kneeling down to a wooden box in the gallows.

I heard the song of death coming from the shallows.
Like the valley before kings in the land of dead pharaohs
Along the road, a demon whispered, "Hello,
I'll show you the way if you just follow."

I told the gatekeeper, "Please weigh my sorrow.
The happiness I found was merely borrowed.
It has been written that the road to heaven is too narrow.
And in death, our sins will find justice tomorrow."

If I always belonged to the shadows
I could never fly with the sparrows.
With wings broken by the devil's arrows
Destined to be a fallen angel descended down below,
To a skulled fate like the black bird crow!

Forever Like Gold

Inside a beautiful landscaped dream
Sand dunes fill a valley before the kings.
Painted pyramids with eagle wings
Where the ancients bow down to sing.
To a beloved pharaoh and queen

On the earth's vortex lines
Built with stone and lime
The pyramids are perfectly aligned.
To every star with hieroglyphic signs

Then to rest in a tomb upon the time
Where sacred writings of death are inscribed
For only the great is mummified.

To live as immortals through the reincarnation of life
Shadowed by royal curses that lay in wait inside
Where the riddle to wake within the labyrinth hides
Beside buried treasure, never to find

And when the sun would rise
Where the dead now lie
Inside a beautiful ancient dream
Before a sleeping pharaoh and sphinx
With a dust of black for decorated eyes
All would kneel down to sing.

"Arise, pharaoh, wake the great lion to fly.
Journey to the land where the sun cries.
A rebirth of the firebird into the sky
Killing death to reign, as our spirits are alive.
For we shall live forever like gold when we die."

Life

Like a terminal disease of the mind
If unenlightened, you could lose your sight.
If you trip and fall, you will be left behind.
It is said that you only fail if you never try.

Therefore, we get up after we collide.
Carry the weight and take it in stride.
And when we have too much pride,
We would rather be alone and cry.

To be content to never understand why
Our feet are chained, and we cannot fly.
To get into heaven, there is no bribe.
We cannot buy God, for he has no price.

Only the soul, as seen in our eyes
Or what is left of it deep inside?
As death is the only guarantee in life,
We only truly become alive.
Once we accept that, we are going to die!

The Black Horseman

With every sound of his gallop, the clock arm runs to 3.
When the darkest night shadows the one who still breathes
As he travels all mountains and across every sea
Like a crow, the black horseman brings eternal sleep.

Born to life for us, destined to meet
Down in the valley, where no one can speak
We barter coins for our eyes with our souls to reap.
As the ground trembles at the black horse's feet

Death is a war we can never defeat.
When the boat to Hades awaits by the creek
Like wood to a fire, we are what he feeds.
If the scale of our hearts is imbalanced by greed,

We shall be burned to ash with our sins for eternity.
Since death is to all that have ever lived, a true destiny
We can only overcome our fear with heroic bravery.
Cometh the hour in time for the black horseman to visit you or me!

Destiny

A fallen warrior
At war for her testimony
A tormented soul
Haunted by her memories
A broken dream
In a shattered picture frame
A torn wing
Beneath unstitched seams
Father, forgive them.
And please forgive me.
With this blood on my hands
I pray I will live to read.
The last words written in my story,
As I fulfill my destiny!

The Black Butterfly

Riddle me,
Puzzle this,
Can you see?
Do I exist?
Am I free?
Or am I lost?
Imprisoned by a mind that never sleeps,
Am I confined to the cost?
If my cuts are too deep to hide my scars,
Will I still bleed for my past?
Awoke, with a dead heart, am I a corpse?
Will my sins outweigh my cross?
Coexisting in an alternate reality behind the glass
Now insanity seems like greener grass.
In all honesty,
I'll take the loss.
You should not love me.
I am too lost.
Forgive me for all the frost.
I decree, and I endorse
I refuse to live with a mask.
Fighting for peace will only exhaust
With more nightmares than dreams
Am I a ghost?
Now, if I breathe, will I distort?
A penny for all your thoughts,
"Who am I?" you ask,
The black butterfly, who flutters in the dark!

Asphyxia

Staring down at the world from a ledge
Sanity will await me within one step.
It seems I am losing the war in my head.
I have been holding on so long to misconcept,
Now I tend to forget.
I can no longer feel my grip.

Behind the mask lives only pretense.
It seems I have been put to death.
For your freedom to exist
Serving an unjust life sentence

Since your self-preservation will not notice
You put these handcuffs on my wrists.
With no master key and no locksmith
Now I am trapped in a maze with no exits.

Underneath the skin, my truth resists
Being judged and buried for my sins
Since my peace no longer visits,
I am tired of hiding my existence.
For the sake of your own conscience

Out here in the dark waters, falling to the depths
I am now fighting for my life or for whatever is left.
Drowned by these waves, until the ocean sounds deaf.
Now every high tide brings back the voice that once said
I realized so long ago that I had to be dead.
How could I live underwater without losing my breath?

Uncharted River

I awoke in a sandbox at 6 feet under.
On my chest, I still feel the pressure.
Buried alive with the world on my shoulders
Cutting my wings to write with the feathers

Now, how can I blame her?
For not keeping together
Something that will be lost forever
Although I still treasure

Every fallen tear from my mother
The irony seems too clever.
Trying to keep her heart aflutter
When mine has been to the butcher

With a past so dark and bitter
Filled with memories, I pray not to remember.
With a weight that I am still failing to measure
Now I am adding up my life to unbalanced figures.

My mind seems to be in danger.
Unable to distinguish the weather
With the sun dimmed each summer,
Still hidden behind the clouds of winter.

Now it seems so easy to pull the trigger.
Every time I stare into the mirror,
And I sympathize with the stranger.
Falling down the waterfall at the edge of an uncharted river!

Confessions

Staring into the mirror at her own reflection
With one bullet in her Smith and Wesson
As she confronts all of her demons.
"Shut up and just listen!
I demand your attention!
I am so sick of being patient.
I am so sick of being questioned.
Low self-esteem and no self-evaluation
Injecting yourself with venom
Ashamed of all your imperfections
Then bleaching your skin complexion
Adding another toxic layer over depression.
So imprisoned by opinions
And society's expectations
Hiding drug addictions
Haunted by the vision,
Of an armed robbery invasion
A racked gun to envision
Through the window in the kitchen.
Counting life by every second
A police investigation
The ivy to its own poison.
Free will with no freedom
Cooperation or prison?
Aggressive cross-examination
Subjected to mental interrogation
A state witness under no protection
The cost of expectation

Awake in a body bag with the realization
You were merely a newspaper caption.
A traumatic life lesson
Expensive therapy sessions
Too unenlightened to envision
Believing you're the villain
Is spoken into existence.
Now I am done with this discussion.
Remember, I am just an observation.
Behind this glass is only an illusion.
If you are seeking redemption,
Only the truth can release the imprisoned.
A prayer for each curse to be buried with a blessing.
Now be true to yourself and tell me your confessions!"

Save Me from Myself

The road ahead seems so distant.
While I pray for my existence
My demons are too persistent.
Feeding off my borrowed innocence
And I know that when I love, I am not consistent.

I was too young to pay the price for my sins.
And I still live with this consequence.
At war for peace, and still so evident
I am only fighting for my own relevance.
I am too oblivious to this acceptance.

Therefore, I cannot tell the difference.
Between the fallen and the victorious
I live on this battlefield, whether past or present.
And I carry all of my scars as evidence.

I lost myself in the sound of our silence.
Afraid of love, I know I was a coward.
Now I am too proud to talk, so I stay quiet.
Will I be strong enough to break this habit?

Protecting myself against you is only instinct.
Now I am too ashamed to transpose how I think.
Therefore, I self-sabotage until I sink.
Fully aware of the enemy with in
I keep throwing myself into the deep end.
The truth is, I just cannot swim.
It has been so cold and dark in this bad dream.

Would you wake me now if I am sleeping?
I wish I knew that I was breathing.
I wish I embraced every flawed imperfection.
I wish I understood that I am only human.

Could you save me from myself again?
God, please save me from myself, amen!

Goodbye

How do I apologize?
I never knew we were on borrowed time.
Now I'll never see your eyes.
And you will never see the sunrise.
I wish I had realized.
Not to have so much pride
I wish I had told you every time.
You told me that I saved your life.
You saved mine.
I wish that I could rewind.
And when you asked me, what was on my mind?
I would tell you that I felt so blind.
Being apart from you every day and every night
Feeling so numb and paralyzed
Before you, I felt so vacant inside.
And know that because of you, I felt so alive.
Now, when it rains, I look up at the sky.
I wonder if that is when you cry?
I am sorry; I never told you that I
I will love you until my soul dies.
So fly, my angel, fly.
Sleep peacefully in paradise.
Sweet dreams now, my love. Goodnight.
Remember, I always hated saying goodbye!

Heaven

As you lay in a peaceful sleep
We count every flower by your feet.
Now led to God so you could meet
And your destiny may be complete.

With fallen tears, the choir sings
As we kneel to pray before our king,
While you journey beyond the clouds to receive,
Feathers for the most beautiful angel wings.

As you transcend life, your eternity begins.
You will be missed, like every summer and every spring.
Now may God forgive all of our transgressions and all of our sins.
And hear all the prayers of grief whispered within.

While the ocean washes away where your footprints have been
We will always carry you in our hearts, our minds,
and even our dreams.
Now, with every visit from death, we realize life is merely
borrowed again.
And as the hourglass counts down each of our sand by the grain
We should live to fill each blank page with ink from our pen.

Since we all awoke to the inevitability that will always remain,
For our bodies shall return as dust to the earth, and our spirits
to God in heaven!

Unbroken

God, here I am.
I lift my hands,
Up to heaven
You call my name
When the devil calls my sin
Then you give me wings.
And save me from my demons.
So I will pray, and I will sing.
Because I am known to him

When I was in the dark
And I only felt a fire burn.
You woke my heart,
And I felt every thorn.
Amidst adversity to overcome
You made me a queen,
And you gave me my crown.
When I was down
And all hope was gone.
You lifted me up to your throne.
You never gave up.
Even when I was done,
Because only you loved me before I was born.

I now realize,
I am unbroken in your eyes.
And forever in life,
I will be unbroken to my king!

Saving Grace

Dear God,
When lost in the dark
I only hear your voice.
When the mountains broke my faith
Upon me, you would always shine your face.

When overcome by the storms and swept away
You lift me up until I can walk on every wave.
Even when I never gave you the praise
You still remembered my name.

Indebted forever, and I could never repay
You still save my life every day.
This truth, the enemy could never erase.
You love me in all my different color shades.

You forgive all my flaws and never let them taint.
The promise of the rainbow that you still paint
Your love for me is so brave.
You take every burden, and in exchange
You bring peace to my heart and numb all of my pain.

Upon my every call, you never hesitate.
Throughout my life, you have always stayed.
Even when I let myself fade,
You still never let me break.

My sanctuary, with you, I am safe.
Therefore, I am not afraid.
If I close my eyes and I never wake
I know you will meet me at the gate.

Forever grateful I just wanted to say,
I am blessed with every breath I have to pray.
In your hands, I entrust my spirit today.
Thank you for always being my saving grace!

Deaf Praying

Deaf praying
In faded dreams
With hope, that disappeared.
She wondered,
"How did I find myself here?"
As the darkness surrounded her
The frontline nears
Alone, facing the enemy spears
Engulfed by the flames of her own fears,
She then prayed and found only her tears.
And when to God she would surrender,
He gave her the power of only her words.
She soon realized that this empowered her.
To not only survive, for she would also conquer!

Spring

Valentine

To my dearest Valentine,
I have been sentenced for your crime.
When you kept your heart and stole mine,
You have now become my lifeline.

Seek me, and you shall find
A love that could have us both so blind
If only you would gift me your time.
We could be the beauty of fate's design.

With a vacant room in my mind,
Open the door and step over the line.
As our energies become entwined,
Finding a love for our souls to refine,

We should light up the sky and let it shine.
Watch if our destiny and our stars align.
We could fall into a love so undefined.
Sincerely yours, forever, Valentine!

Cardiac Arrest

Could you be an angel?
Could you be hell?
Would you be real if I fell?

Could you be a star?
Could you be a scar?
Would you be the truth if I gave you my heart?

Could you bring me war?
Could you bring me peace?
Would you let me fall 10,000 feet?

Could your heart be filled with vengeance?
Could you be the art of beautiful essence?
Would your love paint me in shades of happiness?

Would you give me breath?
Could you give me death?
Or will you be my downfall, like a cardiac arrest?

Beautiful Sin

Hello, it's me again.
I am still so lost within.
Our stolen moments
Listening to the rain,
As our hearts beat to content.
Existing in such a beautiful dream.

I am in love with the feeling.
Of feeling,
You breathing
Softly onto my skin.
And the sound of you inhaling
All of me, deep within.
Then pause before exhaling.
So I can feel you down inside my veins.

Lost in our stolen time
A secret that no one can find
In this moment, your kiss is only mine.
And with every touch, you make me so blind.

In this truth, I cannot lie.
Off of you, I get so high.
I wonder if, in another life,
Her ring would make me your wife?

Now vulnerable and compromised
With all this guilt I feel inside
And it just kills me every time.
I see a love for me in his eyes.

As our secret shall awaken the dead
I pray for my heart to soon pretend.
Keeping you hidden only in my head
If we found a love that was never meant
Why am I still dressed in your scent?
Could I sincerely still love him?
While in love with you, my beautiful sin!

Envious

I envy the way you look at her.
It reminds me of when we were together.
I envy the ring you put on her finger.
It reminds me that you are now gone forever.

I envy the way she holds your heart.
It reminds me that we grew so far apart.
I envy how she lit up your dark
It reminds me that I let you fall too hard.

I envy how she makes you smile.
It reminds me that I haven't for a while.
I envy how she makes you happy.
It reminds me that your happiness was invisible to me.

I envy her for being the better woman for you.
I envy how she made you a better man, in truth.
I envy how you're not sad and blue.
And I am envious, because I still love you!

Love Letter in A Glass

Down at the harbor on an old sailing boat
The wind brings a storm stronger than the docked ropes.
Standing before a high tide with waves that never broke
I still often see the haunting face of your ghost.

When the dark of the night falls upon me with frost
I lay my broken heart at the feet of the cross.
The ocean can be so unforgiving to the lost.
We are destined to capsize within this forecast.

Insanity seems like such an expensive cost.
As your voice finds my ears through the fog,
Asking me the questions I could never ask
"Do you still have shelter in your heart for my love?"

Set to burn out in the sky as the stars
Our destiny has now become our past.
It seems too late to take off our masks.
Forever fated into the ocean to be cast
Adrift, like a love letter stuck in a glass!

Insomnia

I am too afraid to fall asleep.
I still see you when I dream.
Every night, I fall so deep.
I miss the way you breathe.

Lost in the beauty
Of every dream and each memory.
I pray not to wake too easily.
I fear that you will leave.

I wish you would be more discreet.
It's crazy how I still hear you speak.
Your voice still makes me feel so weak.
It echoes in my mind like a stampede.

I know we have long been buried.
Therefore, I would not even plead.
Undone within our closure, and it seems
There are still answers I may need.

When I lose blood, do you also bleed?
In truth, what I am trying to ask is
Are you also afraid to fall asleep?

Bullet

I light a candle and put it underneath the window.
I hope it helps you find your way back home.
I find solace in listening to your favorite song.
I still smell your favorite t-shirt every day that you are gone.

I need to look into your eyes now.
Tell me you are done.
When you look into my eyes, how
Could you not count?
All the tears that have drowned.
There was a time when you loved me like I was the one.
And every day I prayed our love would live on.

I wish that I could talk to you, if only just once.
When you loved me, I felt like I was someone
You had me so high, you took me up to the sun.
You closed my eyes, and now I still see no one.
You inhaled my soul, and now to you I still belong.

Tell me where you are, and I'll leave everything and run.
This distance grows each day that I am alone.
It feels like I have been cold for far too long.
Though I know the worst is yet to come,

Now every time I turn back for you, I turn to stone.
It feels like this mortar is weighing me down.
To live a life of victory without you on the throne
Will bring me no glory or justice to my crown.

If love is a game of Russian roulette, then surely you have won.
As it seems, you are the next bullet in the chamber of my gun!

Suicide

I miss the shades of color in your eyes.
I wish I told you that it kept me alive.
Then I fell in love before I ever realized
Thus, I never had the courage to say goodbye.

I hate that you found happiness with time.
This thought is taunting to know when I am dying.
I still wish you all that is beautiful in life.
Even though you will no longer exist in mine,

I am just alongside a road with painted lines.
Reminiscing on a journey with no lights
I often hear your voice resonating in my mind.
You still haunt me in my dreams at night.

You are attached to my soul deep inside.
Now I still feel every tear that you cry.
Please acknowledge me; I am still waiting outside.
Or do you still feel it is safer to hide?
I just need the acknowledgment without the pride.
Why does my love for you feel like suicide?

Pseudonym

There was once a season.
Whether summer, winter, spring, or autumn
When all things here would blossom
Now this land has become so barren.

Buried south-west, in a box of wooden
Once a vision of the world's most beautiful garden
Now filled with only grains and grains of golden
And like the flowers, all of our dreams were stolen.

The only rain now is from the tears no longer hidden.
As we pay for our hope and our thoughts with a token
The longing for the happiness of when we were children
Only now remains in this desolate land of the broken.

Could we find our way back to the beginning?
Will the unspoken words be spoken?
Or will we keep ignoring our own wisdom?
Existing only in our hidden identity as a pseudonym.

Cold Case

In the attic of her heart
Hides a vintage tintype portrait
Underneath the golden stars
Once enclosed, though now afar,

In a lifetime before the dark
Long before it all fell apart
It was the essence of such beautiful art.
Perhaps it was painted too fast.

The debris of her scattered past
Now buried in a wooden box.
To commemorate a love that was lost
In her summer, at times, she can still feel the frost.
And she still feels the cold-wintered love of her ghost.

Dissect

As my teardrops fall onto an empty bed,
I know my silence never said
I would walk down the valley of death.
For you, if you needed my breath

I would live forever among the dead.
For you, if only for a day to forget
All the scars that I now regret
All the wars and bloody footsteps

How I damaged our love with neglect
And how you were too proud to lose to reject
Now all we are is a memory in my head.
A riddled enigma buried beneath a complex percept

We let our promises die to protect
Our egos and self-intellect
Would always trump our love and respect.
We destroyed each other until there was nothing left.
Now our love is a rotten corpse that we can never dissect!

The Dead

There is no vacant place in my head.
While there in your eyes lingers only regret.
Have I not paid for all of my debts?
When there was no word left unsaid,

If I have loved you in the past tense,
You overestimate your own relevance.
For this love has no substance.
All I feel now is reluctance.

There is no love lost in our distance.
You are not in my subconscious.
Please understand and respect
When we die, we bury the dead.

The Graveyard

Hollow footprints lead down a path.
To echoed whispers faintly heard
The blue skin and the iced bones are hard.
Too numb to feel this winter, or even the summer that had past.

Erasing the stars only to grasp,
The sun was never buried beneath the grass.
Now, with the sound of such a lonely laugh
Engulfed in memories that will better outlast
All dawning on you in outcast

Knocking on the wood in the dark
Still searching for ghosts to put in your glass.
While I have been dead, here in this box
You, a true hunter, are out collecting hearts.
Returned for mine when it had been lost.

Arriving home from a lifetime of war
Unexpectedly to stand before
Latched doors and healed scars
Only to realize the dead and undead all live apart.

Now unseen, muted, and unfelt
You know how it feels to be broken and unmasked.
As you find yourself in solitude, alone in our graveyard!

No Sympathy

You were my air, my every breath.
I loved you like I knew of death.
I went to war for you until I was dead.
I gave my life for you with no regrets.

I sacrificed my peace for you to rest.
Each time you wounded me, I never left.
I gave my heart and soul for us to exist.
Broke down every wall when you would resist.

Then you abandoned me.
And seemingly forgot what you said.
Every time I begged you not to leave,
You pretended to be deaf.
You turned your back on me,
Like we had no depth!

You never cared about me.
And it never existed in your head,
If I was unhappy
Or strong enough to live
You repaid me with no pity.
You showed me no empathy.

Now you want my love unconditionally,
Saying forgiveness will renew our memories.

Well, I say cry.
Until all the oceans rise,
And till all the tides are high.
Cry as I have cried.
Like all the rivers were dry,
As if no rain ever fell from the sky.

Cry for as long as I have cried.
Until all your tears have died.
Cry for as long as you have eyes.
Since no sympathy is left for you in mine!

Crying Wolf

Remember when you said I would never leave?
All the times you would go out and cheat?
Cut me just to let me bleed?
Then watch me cry myself to sleep.

Let me fall just to say I am in too deep.
You said that without you, I wouldn't breathe.
Said, My love for you made me weak.
And because of you, my heart could beat.

Then, finally, you found defeat.
When love puts you on your knees
As karma spun 360 degrees
And all of those seeds
Sowed, you would reap

Now resurrected from the dead
You apologize and plead
Then beg for my love and my belief,
When I no longer feel the grief.

You were cut out like a disease.
And now that I am finally free,
From the shackles you put on my feet
You're a mistake that I will never repeat.

Now all you found in me was the brutal truth.
There is no beauty in the irony of being a crying wolf!

Mr. Narcissist

Out in the world, that seems far too small.
With an ego so big, you're bound to fall.
Hang up the phone before we end the call.
Insinuate the privilege to have your love out of all!

Staring intensely into your favorite mirror on the wall
While you powder your nose and worship the doll.
As you grin, you exert your authority and control.
Perhaps I will always be too short, and you will always be too tall.
A redundant existence that is now so predictable

Flamboyantly tailored suits in an exotic rental car
Hiding an inferiority complex, like primer, over a scar
While high on power and status, like an expensive cigar
Reminding common gold fish that you are caviar
Counterfeited as your clothes, you're truly a mirage.

The life of the party, illuminating every disco ball
Telling your dramatic tales of untrue windfalls
Upstaging any for audience applause
An artificial victorious king, always at war

Now a welcomed standing ovation for you, Caesar!
Believing your hidden persona was inhumed in the dark
An unapologetic narcissist, enlightened, now I know who you are.
Entitled and self-absorbed, with as much gas as the stars!

Summer

The Cape Troupes

The foreign flags of the Dutch colonized her soil in 1652.
As Cape storms brought ashore the slavery of white, orange, and blue
Dehumanizing imports and indigenous natives from the
coastal groups
To oppress their freedom and rights as caged animals in a zoo

To exert political control over the land and their lives with
a racist rule
Intending to fracture their minds and break their cultural views
Reinforcing fear with the whip for labor where death looms
Thus allowed the dictating over the shackled, unarmed, bleeding,
and bruised

In 1674, permitted slaves performed in festivities when every year
was a new
Mocking their masters with ridiculed entertainment, becoming
more resentful
And when 1838 brought the emancipation of slaves from every
foreigner's book
The seeds planted in this tradition had already grown deep
descendant roots.

Adopting a culture that was influenced by European and
American troupes.
The eccentric attire of top hats and tailcoats, with every face
painted so colorful
The live bands paraded the streets of the Cape along
the historical route.

With theatrical dance performances stomping to African drummed tunes
Marching from District 6, strutting through the upper Cape, and ending on Rose to view

A tradition was born on the second New Year, January day number two.
The slaves celebrated their resilient fight for freedom and became immortal.
Outliving the eras of slavery, segregation, and apartheid by dying for their truth,
The iconic survival of the Cape troupes is authentically beautiful!

Set Me Free

Set me free, like my ancestors, from slavery.
Set me free like those captured who died with dignity.
Set me free, like I am a slave ship munity.
Set me free, like the sand beneath my feet.
Set me free like the brave African slaves who walked into the sea.

Set me free, like democracy.
Set me free, like human rights in 1993.
Set me free, like the oppressed, from the apartheid regime.
Set me free, like I am a human being.

Set me free from society.
Set me free from the color within my identity.
Set me free from their racist mentality.
Set me free from the irony.
Set me free from being shackled and still enslaved to humanity.

Set me free because I am owed equality.
Set me free because the lock on my mind has no key.
Set me free because you have no deed of sale for me.
Set me free because I want my liberty.

Set me free because I would never live on my knees.
Set me free, because I am a gladiator who has won my freedom with every defeat!

Silence

In her silence
She escaped the violence.
As she embraced the violins
No longer conscious of her sins

When the world was quiet,
In her beautiful riot
She became so biased.
And cut out all toxic influences.

Shifting her universe like telekinesis
She was her own thesis.
As she puzzled all of her broken pieces
Evolving into a different species

Realigned with the ancient giants
She mastered all of her energies.
Studying all of the science
She distinguished all of her inner fires.
Empowering her spirit to cultivate true love and happiness!

Victory

When I am broken, I stand tall.
I am awakened after each fall.
When I'm weak, I'm still alive.
Like a beast, brought back to life

I am the hunter for my tribe.
The queen lion, of the pride
With ancient animal eyes
Killing my demons to survive
With every enemy sacrificed,

I am a giant, and I am a soldier.
I am a defiant sacred warrior.
I am immortal with each conquer
Like a cannibal, feeding off my own power

Forever to live in my truth, seeking no glory
Fearlessly waging my life to be in the hands of victory!

Champion

I am a storm.
I am a hurricane.
I was born with
A warrior's name

I am the ocean.
And every high tide
I am a stallion.
And the strength beneath its hide

I am an eagle in the sky.
I am a gale-force wind.
I am death, and I am life.
I am like an albatross with powerful wings.

I am her conscience.
I am her sin.
I am the darkness living within.
I am the loss before every win.

I am a devil in hell.
I am an angel in heaven.
I am an undefeated giant.
I am a gladiator in a stadium.

I am a queen.
I am a lion.
Destined to war beside legends,
Living to die with the heart of a champion!

Powerful

Down there on the coast dunes
Underneath the white and blue
Beyond the misty morning dew
Lays foot prints leading to her truth

Broken chains that bound the two
To survive in life like warriors do,
As she fought for her freedom to
Break her silence, which seemed overdue.

With burnt and broken wings, she flew
Battling against monsters, giants, and even a ghoul
Covered in ash from her hell, she knew
She stands victorious in her virtue.

There on the shoreline, gazing out at you
Amidst the rogue waves, her scars also grew.
She now realizes an ocean in turmoil is more beautiful.
And thus, all of her storm tides have only made her more powerful!

Alive!

A haunting darkness stained the beautiful sky.
As the soldier lay infected with a poisonous snake bite,
Now hunted by the devil and the fire in his eyes
Then fed on by demons and vultures like parasites

The enemy's attack of war submerged her life.
Tattooed with her scars to break her spirit and pride
Then abandoned by death and even suicide
As the flames of hell seemed her only light

She prayed for forgiveness, God's favor, and sight.
As she claws out of the pit, wounded and paralyzed,
She then fought for her soul, which could never be priced.
And the cost of her heart was her true sacrifice.

While burning her bones down to ash, her enemies harmonized.
Then, like a phoenix engulfed in the flames, she would rise.
She had no mercy as she set her truth alight.
And she killed every enemy with their own lies.

To end the war, she was powerful enough to say goodbye.
Thus, she chose herself, and she chose to be alive!

Bibliography

Bibliography:

Thomson, Chantal, and Poetry Institute of Africa. Shattered Pillars: An Anthology of African Verse. Scottburgh: Poetry Institute of Africa, 2003.

Footnote: Roberts, 'Untitled', 121.

Bibliography:

Thomson, Chantal, and Poetry Institute of Africa. Silent Skies: A Book of Verse from Young South Africans Aged 13-18 Years. Port Shepstone: Poetry Institute of Africa, 2004.

Footnote: Roberts, 'Unique is a Degrade', 389.

Bibliography:

Thomson, Chantal, and Poetry Institute of Africa. Trials and Tribulations: An Anthology of African Verse. Scottburgh: Poetry Institute of Africa, 2003.

Footnote: Roberts, 'I Mourn You', 157.

www.ingramcontent.com/pod-product-compliance
Lightning Source LLC
Chambersburg PA
CBHW060420050426
42449CB00009B/2041